Disney

Tim Burton's The Nightmare Before Christmas

COLOURING BOOK

First published in the UK in 2021 by Studio Press,
an imprint of Bonnier Books UK,
4th Floor, Victoria House, Bloomsbury Square, London. WC1B 4DA
Owned by Bonnier Books,
Sveavägen 56, Stockholm, Sweden

bonnierbooks.co.uk

Printed in the China
4 6 8 10 9 7 5

008 0622

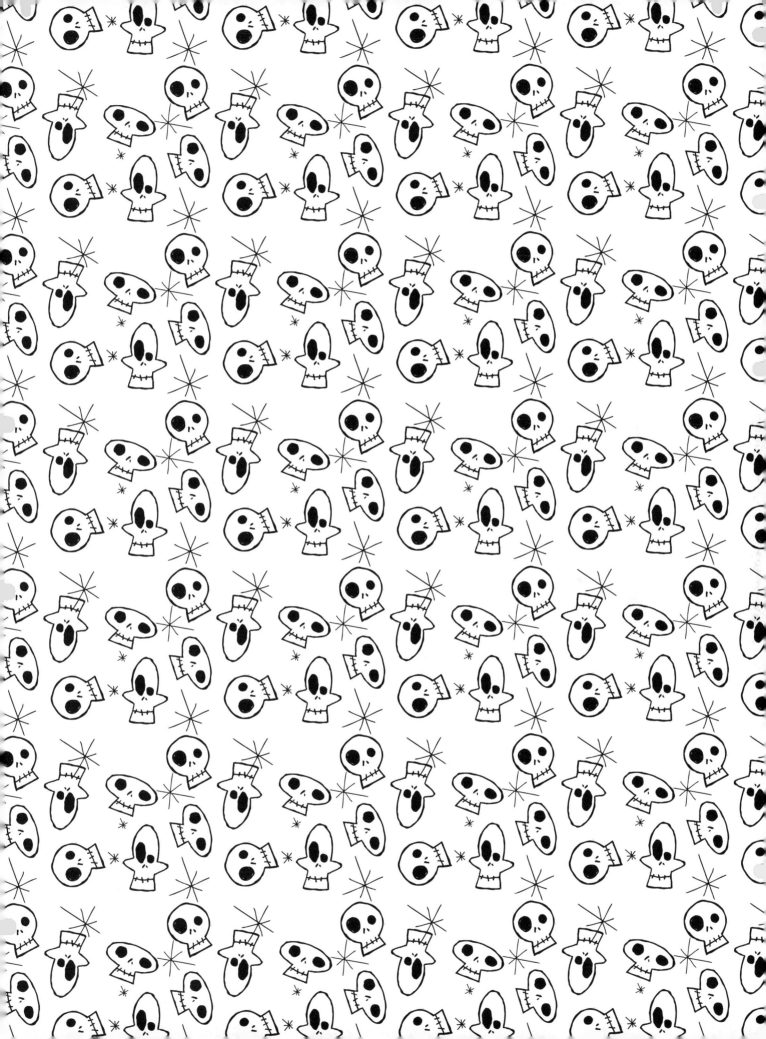

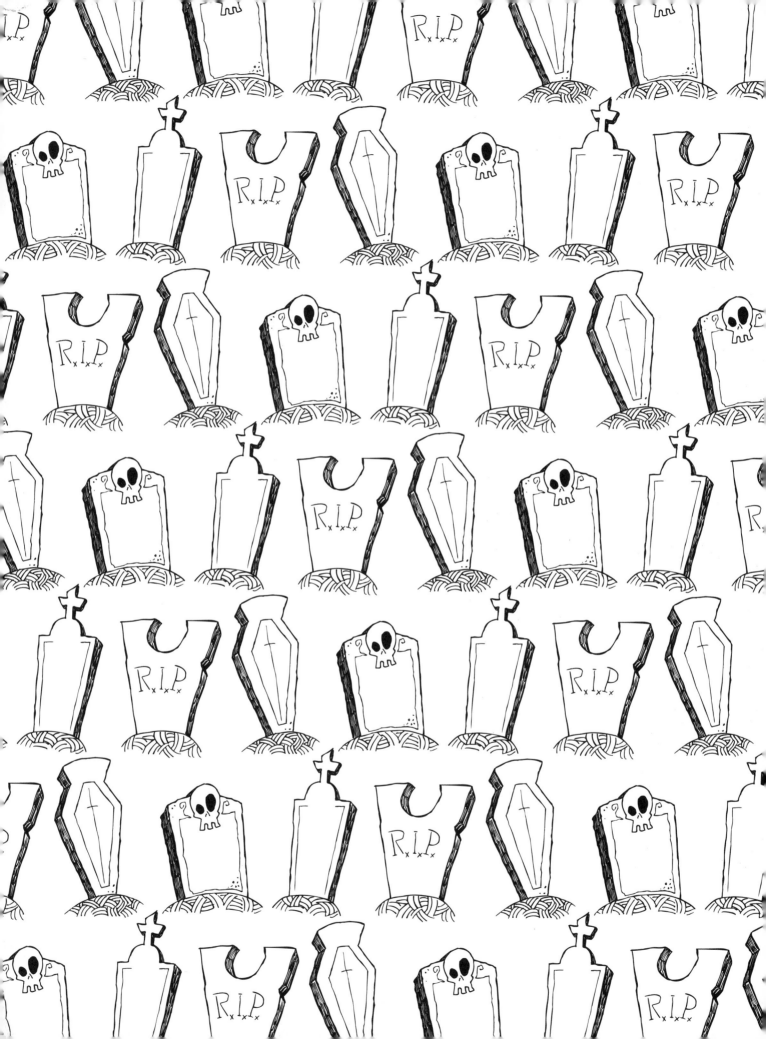

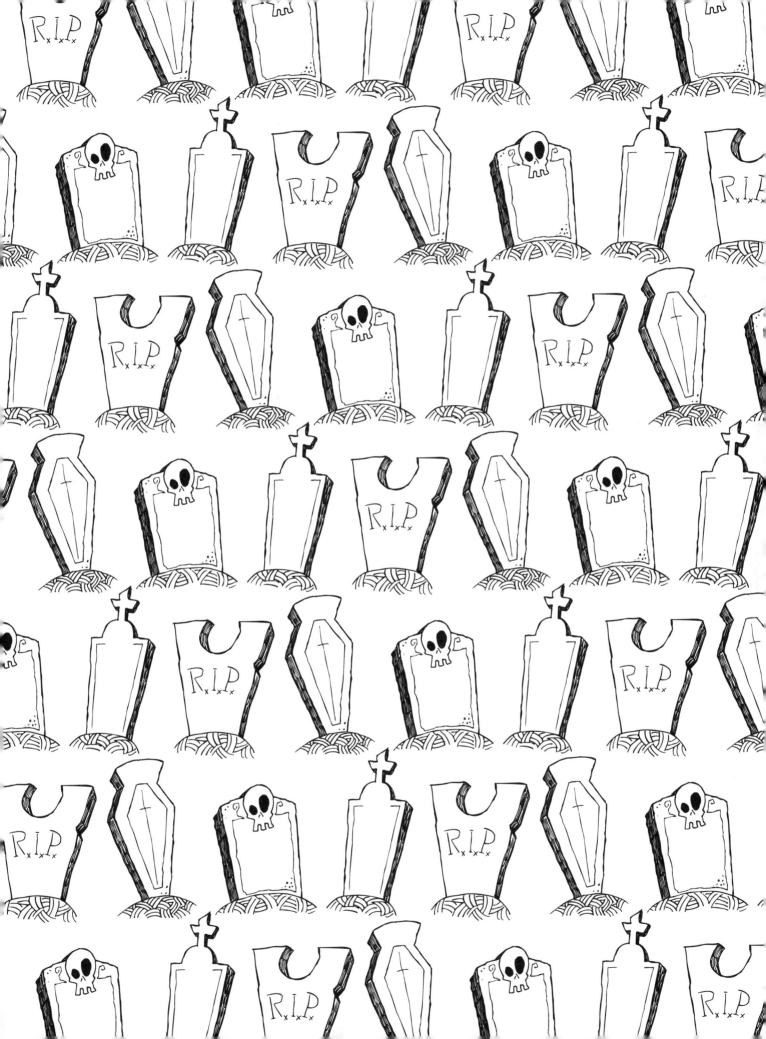

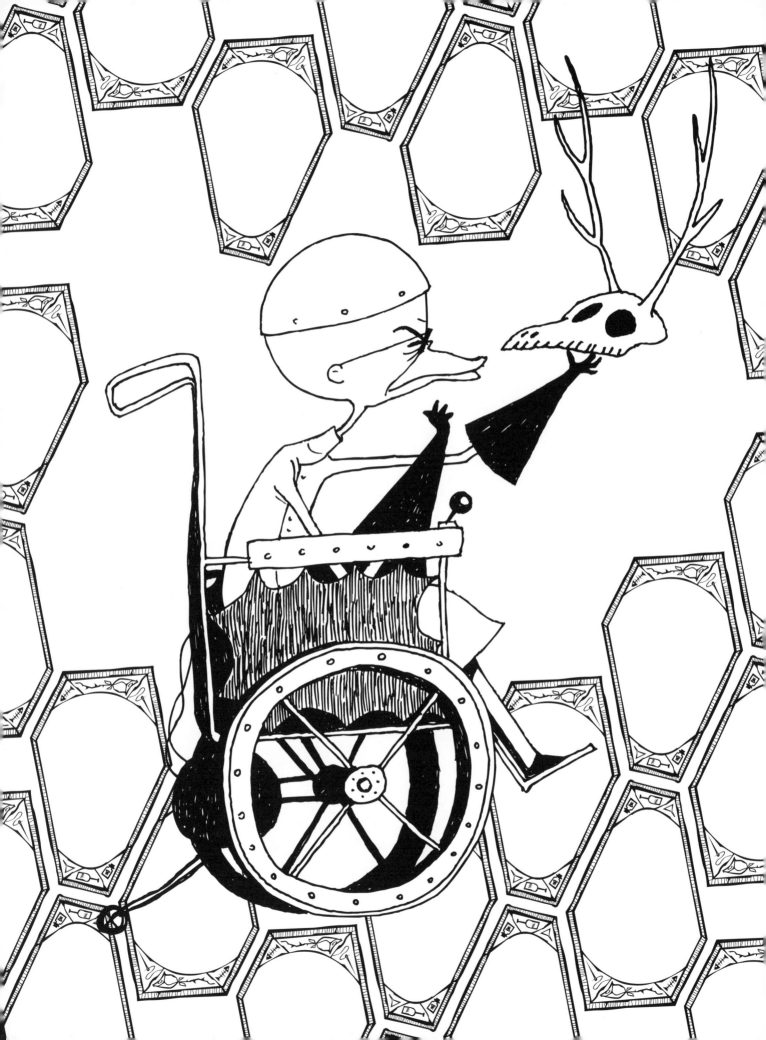

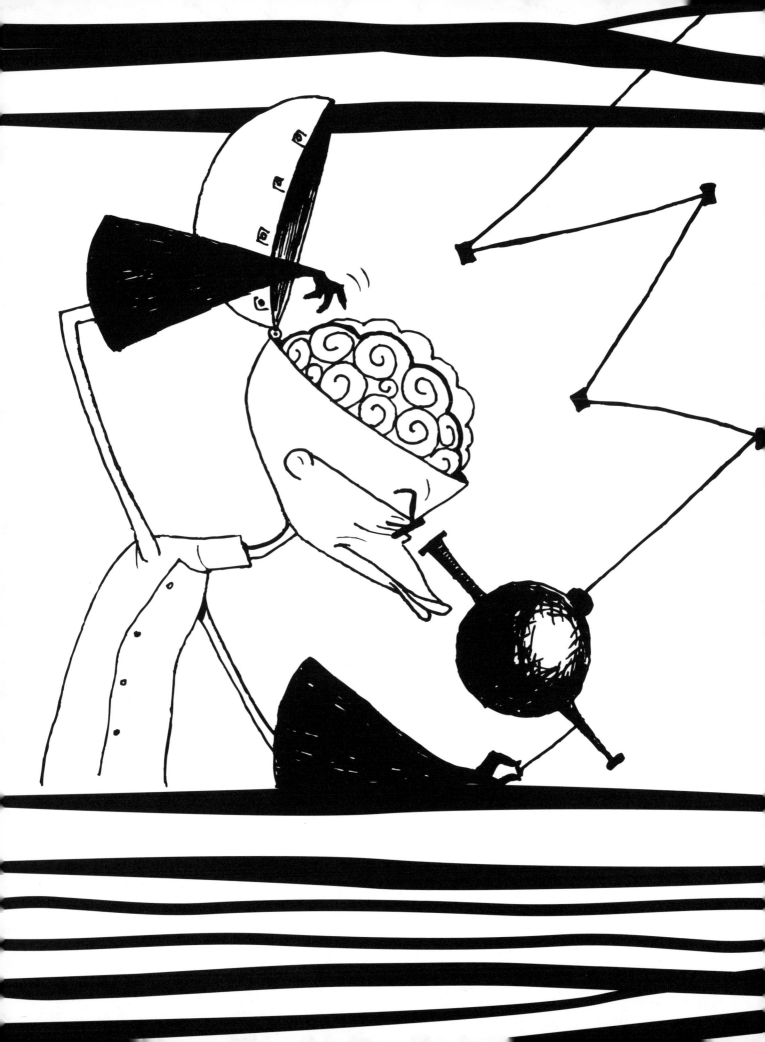

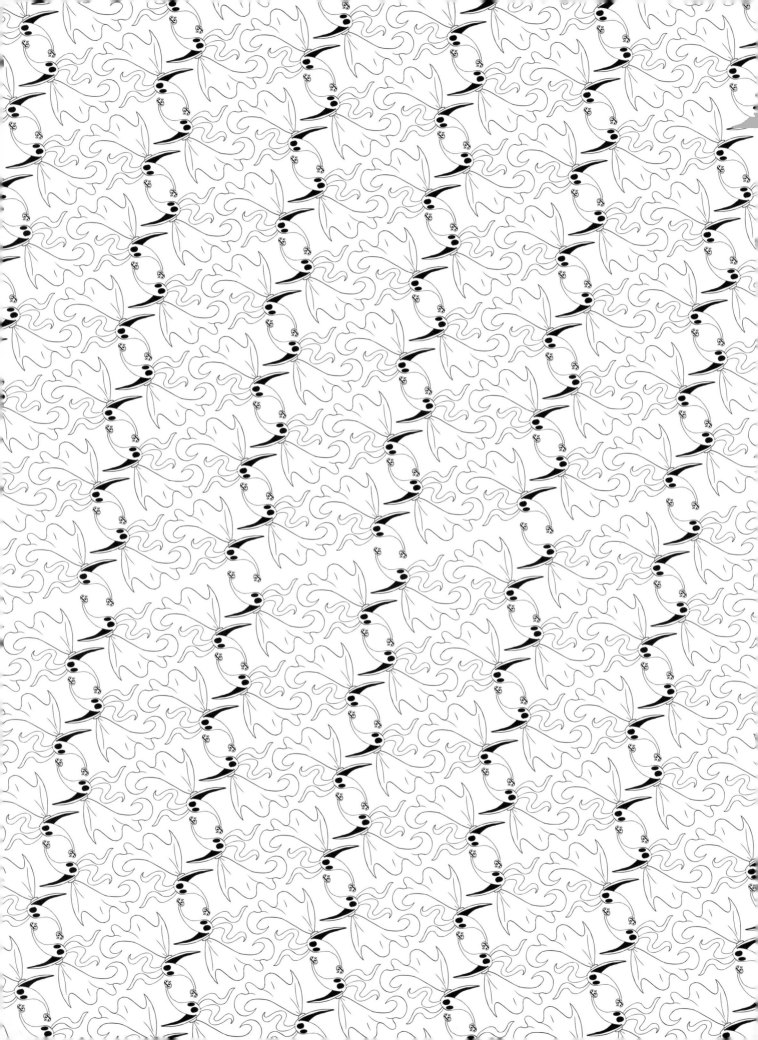

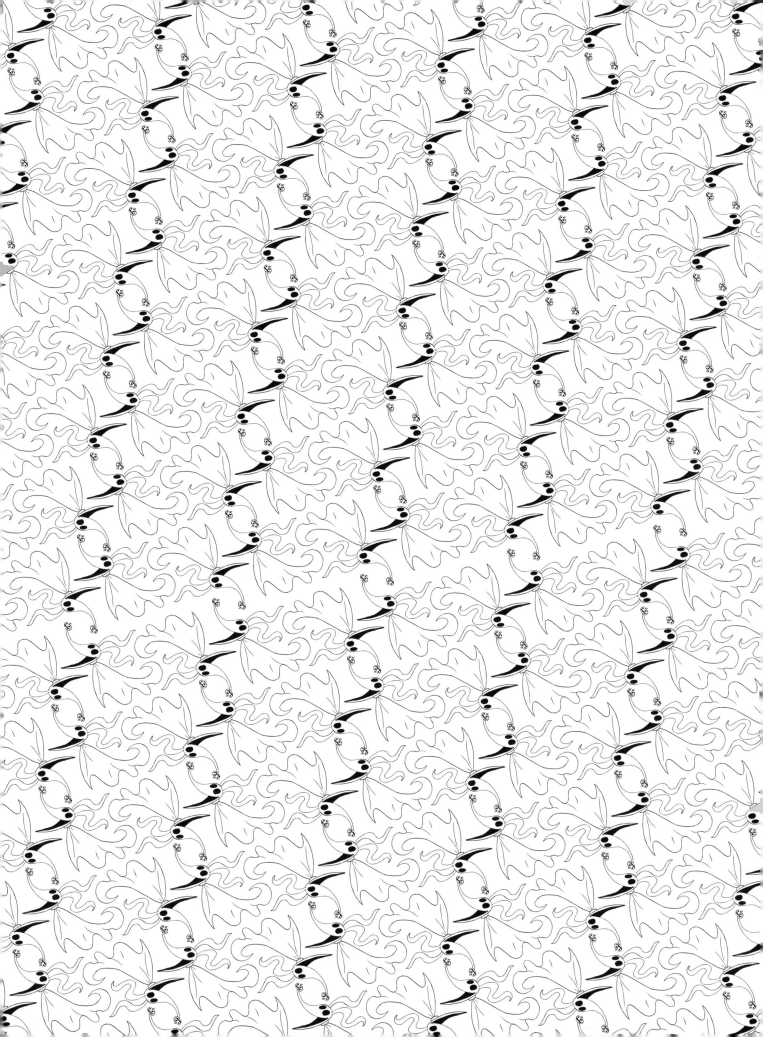

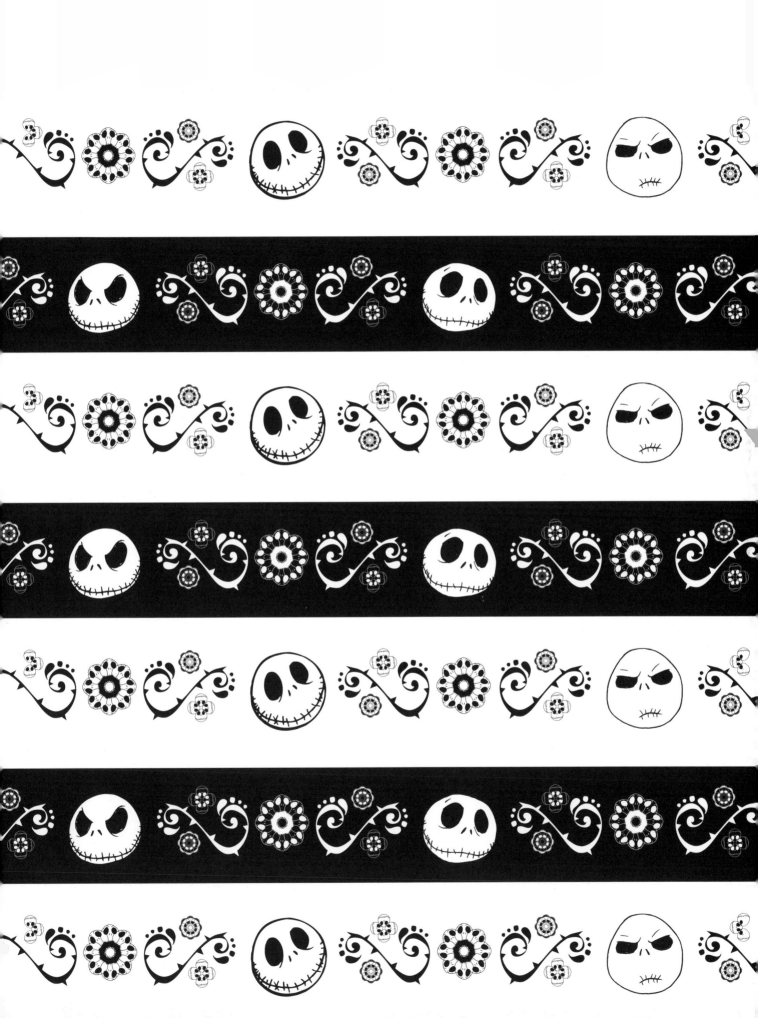

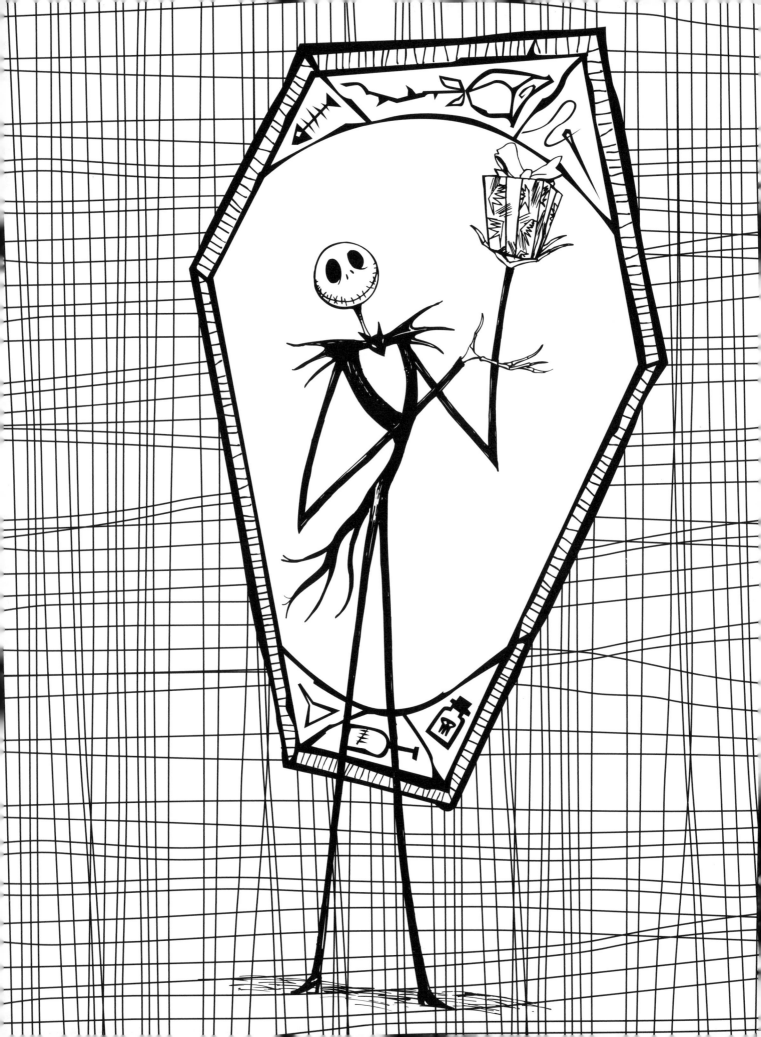